Her Sea-filled Arms:

Layers of Blue

poems by

Magdalena Hirt

Finishing Line Press
Georgetown, Kentucky

Her Sea-filled Arms:

Layers of Blue

Copyright © 2023 by Magdalena Hirt
ISBN 979-8-88838-250-9 First Edition
All rights reserved under International and Pan-American Copyright Conventions.
No part of this book may be reproduced in any manner whatsoever without written permission from the publisher, except in the case of brief quotations embodied in critical articles and reviews.

Publisher: Leah Huete de Maines
Editor: Christen Kincaid
Cover Art: Magdalena Hirt
Author Photo: Magdalena Hirt
Cover Design: Elizabeth Maines McCleavy

Order online: www.finishinglinepress.com
also available on amazon.com

Author inquiries and mail orders:
Finishing Line Press
P. O. Box 1626
Georgetown, Kentucky 40324
U. S. A.

Table of Contents

Cerulean

Crossing from the Canary Islands to Cape Verde

Navy, Aquamarine, & Sapphire

Crossing the Atlantic: From Cape Verde to St Lucia

Indigo

Crossing from St Lucia to Antigua: Caribbean Island Hopping

Azure

Crossing from Antigua to Sint Maarten: Caribbean Island Hopping

Space

Crossing from Sint Maarten to Dominican Republic

Cobalt

Crossing from Dominican Republic to Rio Dulce, Guatemala

for grandmother moon

Cerulean

Crossing from the Canary Islands to Cape Verde

Slip Towards and Under

The half moon like Biden's smile
is stuck in Leo's throat tonight,
but it gives a smooth light
on the waves that gently slide
us south. There's a feeling in the air
with the wind that caresses my hair
from my eyes. Our new head sail
thunders as it fills and spills
with waves. I can breathe.
All our preparations hang—ripe
treasures of land. The ocean is nice
at the moment. A freighter's lights steer
close and cut in front of the bow,
and ARC+ lights glimmer like stars forming
our own constellations. The Atlantic
is like a comforting hug. Her kindness
mystifies me. My youngest, Rory, wakes
and whispers my name in the dark.
I cuddle him under some blankets
with a movie. He's too scared to sleep
without me. The waves under the moon
slip towards and under our Westerly,
Selkie, coating her seal skin with home.
I feel the love of sailing again.

Look

Accept it. Peer behind. See the giant wave
crest and break. You are here again. It is dark.
Selkie floats. Trust in that. The moon will sparkle
on the water wall that approaches. Don't look. Look.
Don't deny it. Be present. Here in this movement of place
is home. Earth. Water. Warmth from the boat. Trust
that it works. Believe. This moment with the wind
and water, this moment with the sound of night
rumbling, the stars are watching. Breathe.

Night Falls Through Me

Darkness—moon's eery smile—stars
beyond stars—waves creep in—under—
a storm brews north—it sends messages
with swells that swallow—wind captured—
wing to wing—gliding—rocking—swaying—
south—southwest—forward—circling
the Atlantic—the night falls through me
stoping near my heart—I clip it in—
harness it—breathe—hold on—let go

Nick's Nest

3:15 am, I crawl out of bed,
try for my sea legs, and approach
the ladder to the cockpit. My husband
updates me on wind, boats, and his
night. "Three oranges and lots of
cookies," he informs me. A steady
wet, warm, ocean breeze encircles
the cockpit and takes stories of us
out to sea. He unzips his Musto bibs,
which we call "the sleeping bag pants"
and hands them to me. We exchange
laughs on our state-of-mind, and he
stands to go sleep revealing his nest.
Four foldable, blue cushions are spread
and compressed like a giant bird's nest.
I can't wait to cozy into the space
he has nestled and provides under
the stars, above the water, and through
the night. Our dark bubble of a home.

Decision

The motor hums. Zero wind.
The only thing that is brilliant
is the stars. Thankful for the engine,
but missing the quiet strength
of the wind, I decide not to write,
not to discuss the space of water
that spreads in mystery beyond
the eyes, not to mention the earth
spinning and the stars rotating
in endless beauty, not to tell
that my life feels as vulnerable
as a ripe apple about to drop
from the home it barely grasps.

Kite Sailing

Like a day at the park flying a kite,
except the wind or air just can't quite give
what you want, as if the atmosphere
or gravity weighs too much on almost
a perfect moment. The sails attempt
to fill like the pull of the string in your
hand as you run through the grass,
but the moment you think it will glide
up into the air like a desire to reach
a new place is the moment it comes
crashing down back into earth. No matter
how you jump, throw, or run with it,
the kite seems sad, so you sit, wait,
watch, listen to the fractured peace.

New Moon

Pan Pan, Pan Pan echoes over VHF radio.
The distress call, one click from Mayday
has my husband shaking me out of bed.
17 degrees 34.630' North
24 degrees 26.958' West
"We are taking on water. Repeat.
We are taking on water.
Pan Pan.
Pan Pan."

Second to only fire: Water is the problem sailors
don't want to have. Eighteen miles behind us.
Three hours for *Selkie* to motor against wind
and current. We pull in our sails and prepare
to turn. Kid boat to the rescue. A boat closer
speaks up. All boats fifty miles from Cape Verde
after a seven-day crossing. With worry, we motor
on towards the light of land in the darkness of stars.
We must leave the distress to another in the night.
A new moon makes the darkness thick, but within
the awe, we find each other. Fragile stars that hold
water outside walls that float—a balance. Strangers
turn quick friends in survival mode. Sailing teaches daily.
A lighthouse off of Ilha de Santo Antão spins—beckons:
This passage will end, and a new one begins.

Navy, Aquamarine, & Sapphire

Crossing the Atlantic
From Cape Verde to St Lucia

Lily

Above The Gambia Abyssal Plain,
16,410 feet deep, 16,410 feet of endless
mysteries, and Lily is on watch
in her own darkness that stretches
2,075 nautical miles across the surface
from one volcanic isle to the next,
from Cape Verde to St Lucia. A wave
wakes me, erratic, bigger than the others,
and I sit up with a sharp breath. Lily.
Lily. The waves settle again, and so do
I. Little Mara with her braided hair sleeps
next to me making little content noises
like a hammock sways in a deep wood
with an exhausted, playful child. Big wave,
and I sit up with a sharp breath. Lily.
Lily. I tell myself she's okay. I tell myself
that she does know how to check
the sails, the wind, the boats, our speed,
for squalls. Lily. Just 12. Mystified
under the stars—responsible.

Like a Willow

The breeze from the ocean blows
through me like a Willow tree moving
my long limbs gently and waking
my phosphorous lights. Why the ocean
makes me rooted in movement, only
the deepest part of me knows. I relax into
the feeling, adjust my tiny leaves
on the night, and wait for the warm sunrise.

Thanksgiving at Sea

333 NM sailed. 1749 yet to capture.
Selkie and the stars will be our family
this holiday. Even ashore, Covid
would keep us away, so why not
be bobbing at sea away from football
and drama, away from dishes and...
The turkey would be brining
in the basement fridge. The mothers
would be hovering anxious to help
with sides. The fathers would be
wandering, basting, playing with the kids.
The China on display in the cupboard
would be pulled out for the table,
and the new tablecloth with Fall
colors and stoic turkeys would be pressed
and laid with candles and turkey shaped
butter, but... Here I am. My turkeys
tucked in their beds. No big meals
to make. Perhaps some cutlets
and carrots. Some biscuits and jam.
This Thanksgiving, we will bob and rock
with the waves in the middle of the ocean.
We will know what survival
is, and what it truly means
to need and depend
on each other. We will
remember
and be
thankful.
The moments we will have
will happen in the cockpit
with sleepy eyes and warm
breezes, destinations, memories,
and each other
within 49 feet
inside our vessel
with each other, close
to each other.

Not Tonight

I write tethered in by my life jacket in an open cockpit finding that a notion
of remaining calm in a rogue wave or disaster would be my only answer.
Last night, glowing orbs
under the surface
floated towards
and under us
like a magic,
underwater
Milky Way—
a brilliant
crimson river—
leaving me
with awe
and sublime
terror. I could see
it glowing
in the distance,
then we'd slide
through, then
it would disappear,
then reappear.

Not tonight.

Tonight huge waves like walls approach from behind visible
by an eery moon that lights the clouds and water oily black
and starless gray. My nerves sting and clench. I breathe deep.
Not committed to one jibe sailing directly downwind *Selkie* rolls
port to starboard and back causing the sleepless to grip
onto bed frames, lee-cloths, or shelves. There is a reason sailboats
are filled with railings and strangely placed handlebars.

From mystery
to misery?
Perhaps.

What does the ocean have in mind for us?

Strange lack of control—a genie in a bottle—a climber
without a rope. Will I see reason or feel joy? Not tonight.
But perhaps,
the wind speaks to my ears,
the moon comforts me,
and movement settles me stable
into incomprehensible uncertainty.

First Mate

I am the Momma, me, first mate,
but my 14-year-old son, Tristan,
lacks the confidence in me.
He wakes me at 4 am
for my watch. He points out
a possible squall. "I'll keep
an eye on it," I say. "How about
you help me with the sails?"
Reefed for squalls, his father
has tamed them for his son's
shift, but I don't want training
wheels. I sail. He says, "Daddy,
didn't say to." I laugh. Shake it
off. The little faith in his mom
is due to her time in the galley
feeding him. Now taller than me
with bigger feet, he believes
in our Captain Dad, which he
should, but he doesn't notice
Momma's wind power. Born
from canals and lakes, raised
on the water, I am a sailor. I
release him to dreams and pull
out the sails myself. I aim towards
the setting moon. Orion pops up
out, above my port head sail
as I soar wing to wing, butterfly.
I keep Ursa Major starboard aft,
and I am capturing the ocean
via the stars. He doesn't see.
He sleeps. The wind shifts
20 degrees, I adjust. It shifts back,
I am attentive and I sail to moon
again. I place the waves behind
me, gliding. Another mother sails
behind me with two young children
under seven. We have the night.

They don't see. They dream,
perhaps of their fathers conquering
storms, but Mommas make the potions
they sleep on, weave the wind
they rest their heads on, and sail
the stars they wish on. The moon
falls towards the water. My youngest
son wakes in the dark with growing
pains. I tuck him in, cast a spell, care
for them all as I sail, and know
the magic it takes to be first mate.

Night Squalls

Captain Dad stays up till 4 am
avoiding, sailing through, and battling
squalls. Twinkling crimson blips
on the radar, they inspire awe
then terror. Sails in. Stay sail out.
40 knot winds expected. The moon,
almost full, turns the night to day,
but the black wall squall could ruin
a lot of things. After two days of insane
waves, the ocean is no longer confused.
She's having fun with us sprouting
her squall babies here and there.
She lays her rain and wind nests
like eggs to crack. A week deep into
the Atlantic, the diesel remains unused.
Selkie sails her ass off. Proven to be
a member of the family with her safety,
we hold fast to our big girl. Her heavy
haul dreaded in small marina maneuvers
has proven to be loving, comforting,
like a strong hug from a mother. Sky
goes black, moon gets swallowed, rain
plays in the air. That dark wall is not
on the radar. Wind picks up. Wind turns.
Wind dies down again. Moon returns.
Waves push me towards the next
system. Trust 260 degrees. Pointed
south of St Lucia, we must ride this out,
wait it out, let the squalls have their way,
then work north on a sunnier day. Stars
stay with me. Moon come back. Give me
a steady breeze, dependable. Nope.
Sky goes black. Ocean peace not visible.
Is there another side? A way out?
A moment. Wind and water settle.
A breath. Moon blots out. It begins
again. A push. A pull. A curious stillness.

We are a small toy boat for the ocean
tonight. Clear over there. Not over here.
The elements play hopscotch on top
of us, splash us this way then that.
Jumping. Tossing. Caught. Sailing.

Last Night in November

And then it was calm.
The ocean settled into
small movements. The sails
made more noise waiting
for wind than the ocean
and all her life. *Selkie*
creaked slow under moonlight
like a woman tanning
in the sun. Shh. She's quiet.
The night, a moment, this life
has not seen in a long
time. Sails shutter. Sails
fill. Small swells smooth
us along the surface west
into moonlight on the water,
like a path already laid,
a yellow brick road. Looking
to bow, the Genoa glows
like a night light. In the distance,
the wind howls like a wolf, but not
here. Here it tickles my face
lightly speaking in whispers.

Full December Moon

The light tames the water and wind
into a whisper, a lullaby. A northeast
breeze warm and filled with memories
walks us along the surface southwest
captured just slightly with our deep
purple code zero—full and almost
weightless. The full moon's rainbow
colored aura looks like a second sphere
calling *Selkie* onward like a siren
in the sea, like our trail could possibly
lift in the atmosphere and float off towards
her like a children's book, like a dream.
Bright, we are held to each other
in an endless dark space, partners
holding hands—sea settled, a blanket.
A line squeaks like a playground swing,
and I am transported to nights on land
under a full moon. My mother holds
my hand storytelling on a neighborhood
walk, my college legs pump contemplating
dirt—earth, my hands push the backs
of my children rhythmically through
the years. A lightweight water gravity
brings me back, and I am sailing quietly,
not disturbing the delicate balance.

Halfway

I wake
dreaming
of poets
halfway
to somewhere
in their lives
reading
poetry
in a green
space
comforting
each other
enjoying
words.
I'm halfway
in the blue
moon-filled
night
water
lapping
the haul—
thirsty
tongues,
and me
barely
moving
into what
I should
be, unless
I'm already
here.

With the Moon

With the moon, I can see
the mystery. It builds white,
gray, mountainous in the light.
Flat bottomed, it drops rain,
sucks up the wind holding
you still, then keeps you
trapped inside with its power.
With the moon, I can see
it approach—a monstrous,
fluffy shape that will swallow
me vulnerable on the ocean
like a hungry tiger, I can see
light inside it, light in its eyes,
ravenous energy. It approaches.
Prepare to pull the main sail in,
it's almost on top of us. Patience.
A bit of horror. A bit of awe. Nature
pairs us both in this moment. Wait.
4 miles. 2 miles. Air stops. Sails bang.
Moon disappears stars twinkle out.
Hurry. Close the hatches. My world turns
wet. Wind picks up. Only Venus peers
through. Is she laughing? Is she watching
over me? Overhead, the squall has fun
with me like a child blows on a toy,
the wind changes, sails back, I turn
north 40 degrees. I soar. It pours. I sail
behind following it, exhilarated. Breathing.
The sun rises. The horizon spills
a cinema-colored sky. Not quite
believable. It moves on. Sails bang
confused. Venus still stares. Moon
reappears, and she and I watch
the ocean dance trying to keep up.

Mommy, Mommy

~ a day poem

In constant, and sometimes
simultaneously, I hear requests.
"Mommy, can I have crackers and cheese
with no cheese?" "Mommy, I'm hungry,
but I want to lay down and eat and watch
a movie." "Mommy, is it a school day?
Where's my iPad? Will you play Minecraft?"
"Mommy, where's the glue, scissors,
and paper?" "Mommy, I made this for you."
"Mommy, I don't feel good." "Mommy,
will you make popcorn?" "Mommy,
What day is it?" "Do I smell popcorn?"
"Mommy, bring it here." "Mommy,
are you gonna start school soon?" "Mommy,
if this happens... never mind. I know
the answer." "Mommy, after this can I have
some Sprite?" "Mommy, what are we having
for lunch?" "Mommy, can I make soft pretzels
today? Do we know how to make pretzels?"
"Mommy, will you make me a sandwich?"
"Mommy, look at me! Watch this!" "Mommy,
more cheese." "Mommy, how do you spell
'looking'?" "Mommy, more cheese!" "Mommy,
are you making more cheese?" "Mommy, I just want
to tell you something." "Mommy, pretty, pretty
please." "Mommy, how fast are we going?" "Mommy,
when will we get there?" "Mommy, I'm done." "Mommy, I don't
want to help." Then they notice me, and...
"Mommy, where does this go?"
"Mommy, can I help?"
"Mommy, do you need me?"
"Mommy, what do you want to do?"
"Mommy, only an English major would ask that."
"Mommy, watch this. Mommy. Mommy?"
"Mommy, I love you."

"Mommy, do I have super powers? Am I immortal?"
"Mommy, I know this is a bad time, but where is the coconut chocolate?"
"Mommy, thank you"
"Mommy, what star is that?"
"Mommy, I love you."
"Mommy, can I snuggle?"
"Night,
Mommy."

Marmalade

Sky turns marmalade
like a thick, homemade jam,
and my mind settles cozy
on the ocean. The clouds
resemble a pillow fight
gone wrong—cotton stuffing
finds new places in the room.
Sunrise scares the stars
into hiding, and cerulean blue
blankets of water and air
parallel me to a safe bed
hiding in deep blue covers
of home. Quarter moon
still bright hovers above
the mast and holds me
like magic, like my mother.
In return, I hold my children
snug in beds and blankets
on the spinning ocean.

Decisions

As the chili boils and mixes flavors,
mom and dad with two oldest children
gather in the cockpit to discuss
what's next? Where to? How shall they sail?
Captain throws a curveball saying South
America, Strait of Magellan, Cape
Horn, Patagonia. Silence falls.
Not the plan. Perhaps not the equator's
"coconut milk" route either, not through
Panama. They will go North—either
to Iceland and Faroe Islands—or
the Northwest passage through the ice
and polar bears. Life in constant travel
has life in constant choice
that can change like the weather.
Decisions now are made for family
in the States, the magic pull—
grandparents. The chili is ready, and they
burn their tongues. The Atlantic sunset
screams orange and pink in the west.
And just like that, the wind changes,
decisions are made, and their life
like a warm meal with a cool
breeze, like a flying fish humming
the surface of the deep gives them
a plan, until the light of the next day.

Plans Change

Like surface tension in wind,
cloud bottoms subject to atmosphere,
family relationships in fluctuation,
virus adaptation to exposure,
destination within decision,
and place outside of presence,
plans change.

Wind

He's back stretching the sails,
heeling the hull, cutting us through
waves. *Frédéric Chopin*, another sailing
vessel, plays music with us—7 knots.
We've waited patiently, mid-Atlantic,
for the wind to return, and he falls
through us like shooting stars,
Cupid's intoxicating arrow.

Ocean and Stars Again

~for my Aunt Mary

Awoken from a dream where I stand
in dunes watching orcas jump and play
in a pink mist just for me, it is the ocean
and stars again. A gentle breeze makes us
turn north to keep the sails full. Over
sixteen thousand feet of mystery makes
dreams seem not so far away. Sailing
through the night, through the stars
is like a complicated puzzle with baseball
on the tv in the background, a smoke
resting, burning in its tray, my Aunt Mary
hovering, helping, making life so simple
to enjoy. The ocean like a basket
of ribbons can be unwound and wrapped
around my brother like tales of the sea.
The night sky like a quilt sewn in patterns,
each star a needle's hole, stitch, strength
can be chosen, cut, and placed carefully
together like the design, fabric of water.
Maybe orcas, dreams, and memories
are closer than they feel. Maybe
I can wrap my arms around an orca
in a familiar hug, watch my Aunt's
expression during a Tigers home run,
and pull the homemade quilt over
my little girl legs like pink mist in a sunrise.

Surrounded by Squalls

Selkie drifts—three full sails, poles out
on head and stay, preventer on main.
The sky opens and drops on my starboard
side. Rain sheets the horizons from view
like a great house on the ocean. Hidden
inside one that stretches up like a monster
is a rainbow. A beautiful cyclops, it plays
with us like the food, the sheep, saved
for the morning—tea and biscuits—
hull and sails. My husband wakes, and we
sit in the cockpit to watch the show. Wind
picks up, and we are flying—the cool
breeze is sensual, after hot days bobbing
about the water like lost lambs. Squalls
are shepherds herding us towards home.

Ocean Pull

Do you see the moon smiling? Orion
off the bow? Do you see the night
dark and empty, yet filled with stars?
Can you feel the ocean roll in looking
huge, endless, rocking you to and fro?
Can you hear the sails flap, the water
break, the stars shoot? Does your skin
move with the wind, speak his language?
Can you feel the ocean breathe on your
body? Two weeks, three days at sea, one
hundred eighteen nautical miles to go,
nineteen hundred seventy one sailed.
Do you feel the pull to return already?
Like it's over, but the ocean is not ready
to let you go? Her wetness in the air
tugs your legs, your heart, your soul.
Then I guess you're like me. I guess
you are born from water, wind, the spin
and roll of the blue earth, born to move,
feel, hear, see the water that gave,
and that will take back, the water
that dances your ancestors, the water
that breathes life into you, the water
that begs you to follow and ride
her surface like a free flying fish.

Finish Line

~St. Lucia, Rodney Bay

Pitch black, all hands on, wing to wing,
we soar through the twinkling light
of islands and stars. Plenty of room
seems a myth in the darkness. Land
seems dangerously near, but then
again, it's been so long since
we've come within eye distance.
Time change—life of legs. Depth change—
those of beach goers. We are of wind,
we are of the night waters, moonrise.
One hand on main, other on helm,
eyes to shore—strange curves
that need interpretations. Preparations
discussed—over and over like the rolls
of waves that cheer us on. Pigeon
Island—dark and anxious to call us in.
Hills of bright lights—night life. We bring
our own lights through riptides. Water
that rolls onto shore gently terrifying.
Land masses playing eye tricks.
Distance. Rocks. Shore. Within reach.
A channel by flashlight. Toss the lines.
A stillness. Gravity that doesn't swing.
Dock. Earth. Still. Still. Rum Punch.

Indigo

Crossing from the St Lucia to Antigua
Caribbean Island Hopping

Healing

There's no reflection in the dark
waters tonight. In urge to look inside
myself has me gazing deep between
the stars searching for ways to heal.
Hunted. My own kindness rips flesh,
but the sea is calm. I should be calm.
Tears have been at the ready for three
days dropping easily. Leeward
of Dominica, headed to Antigua,
from St Lucia, Caribbean waters
are gentle with me. Perhaps,
too gentle. A self-destructive part
of me wants to suffer. My sailing
self needs escape, but I have it. Stop
seeking balance. Be aware and accept
being off kilter. Drink some tea. Breathe.
Laugh. The arrows will miss. The sea will
hold me—let me make my own
decisions. New beginnings. Island
to island—at a new anchorage, different
beach, other fish. We drop the hook
under the light of the moon. I crash
the heavy metal into my dim shadow
of a reflection. Hold fast. Breathe.
It will be more defined in the morning.

Azure

Crossing from Antigua to Sint Maarten
Caribbean Island Hopping

Piano

Forward like soft keys
that play the song
that pulls you deeper
equalizing
clearing the fog of the sea
the links of the anchor chain
pull us further. Side by side,
wing to wing, problems
become erratic waves
that surprise and pass. Voice
within reach, space not between
but endlessly, immensely spread above
giving us eons of time. Our sail
flutters, bangs, so does yours.
The sea lulls and tugs. In movement,
we met. In our ingredients, we
keep a solution.

Conversation

The Milky Way breaks
the conversation between
the stars. St Bart's Gustavia
light the low clouds overhead
like the underside of a slow
moving fish that passes
on a deep dive. Our wings
are spread and held in place.
Gently, so gently, we sail
downwind with following seas.
So much life has brought me
to this calm like an aged turtle
that comes up for a breath.
The ocean is an old friend now
that pushes me on the swings,
takes me for walks, and talks
with me about the weather.
I'm grateful my friend is sleepy
tonight granting me passage
with a warm breeze that plays
with my hair. The Milky Way breaks
the conversation between the stars
to tell me it's time to rest my feet.

Space

Crossing from Sint Maarten
to Dominican Republic

With the Stars

I just want to be alone
with the stars.

It's Been Forever

since I've seen this night sky.
Too busy caught In Caribbean
bays like an ostrich with her head
in a hole. The world, the water,
movement, I had been captured.
My seal skin stolen from my selkie
sailing body. Forever bound by
nets that ensnared myself,
my children. My thirst for sea
unsatisfied. I couldn't feel
the wind or see the stars
like I do now. My wandering
killed by notions of togetherness.
Sentiments. I need to be alone.
Balance. Refigure. Re-wonder.
Before I was ensnared by love,
human connection. Tonight
I need to break free. Eventually
a sailor, like me, leaves. A destination
all their own is needed. Astounding—
the feeling of suspension between
sky and fathoms—the back and forth
balancing—calling—centering—
equalizing. Lights on the horizon.
Virgin Islands in the distance. Space
between me, in me, around me—
space that breathes remember,
space that whispers move, space
that calls me forward alone
in the dark—unafraid.

Layers of Blue

Daytime. Wing to wing. Layers
upon layers of blue. A bird
circles us and dives. A child
comes and complains about
another. My fingers are stained
red from a permanent marker
kid picture of a compass rose
on a clementine I peeled. The long
day warms. The breeze
steady. The crescent moonrise
last night lingers
in my mind
smiling at me.

On Mother's Day

From off the north coast, the lights
of Puerto Rico create questions
and curiosity of culture. From here,
they warm my soul as I think
of the cozy beds with mother and child
snuggled dreaming. I'm not alone either,
my youngest woke without my cuddles
and watches a movie just to be near me
in the cockpit. Swaying back and forth
through the night on a deep, dark, calm
ocean that encourages dreams. A squall
passed through. The cushions are damp,
but it's still warm enough for pajamas,
a sweater, a life jacket. Saturn and Jupiter
are behind me in Capricornus, the playful
sea goat, that chases females and takes
siestas. They ride his back, tangled
in his tail, wanting, like me, to know
his secrets. I await the moon. She will rise
an hour before the sun then disappear
giving us another tropical sea sail.
But Puerto Rico will never know me.
I sail past. Destination Samana,
Dominican Republic. Virgo, the Maiden,
daughter of stars and dawn, pulls me
forward towards earth, my own mother.
Overflowing with magic, she will bring
home in her hair, stories in her fingers,
and puzzles on her skin. Time will stop.
I will embrace her with sea-filled arms,
Caribbean flavors, and island moves.
We will hold the jungle, the ocean,
the wind, as we soak in the night air
together under the moon as she grows full.

Lightening

Burst. Flash. Flicker. Light
goes out. Wait. Watch. Burst.
Flash. Flicker. Night ocean image
quickly shared. Burned on the retina.
Squall builds in the dark, port side,
like a wolf in the night. Triple flash.
Out. Glimpses in the deep dark.
Rumble. Lapping waves lick the hull.
Wind stalks. Wolf approaches.
His mouth open. Tongue hanging.
Whole sky turns on! Boom. Silence.
Just a head sail out on a pole.
No stars. Just Jupiter in the mist.
Ominous swells push up, slip under.
Storm on the water. Flash. Flicker.
Approaching Bahia de Samana.
So close. Burst. Flash. Wolf backs
down patient. Pitch black movement.
Sailing. Slowly. Inching towards
safety after three, bright, beautiful
days at sea. This. A juxtaposition.
Wind howls. Wolf calls his pack.
Squall off starboard. Surrounded.
Burst. Flicker. They are tired
of waiting. Lights on! Lights off.
The sky teases. Rumble. Rain.
Flash. Flicker. So close to safety.
Four hours to the first buoy. Land.
The clouds grumble. The wolves
are hungry for a boat like ours.
Streak in the sky. Heart stop.
They've found me. Watch.
Reef in the sail. Pray for the stars.
Darkness you can touch. Moist
on the skin. A small calm before
they're on me. 4 knots to 8 knots.
Lights bright. Flash in my face.

Rain drips down. The wolves'
saliva. Howl. Whistle. Smell
their breath. Chewed. Devoured.
Strange calm in the belly.
Focus. Speed. Riding. Pulled.
Endure. Prepare the lines. Sail.

Cobalt

Crossing from Dominican Republic
to Rio Dulce, Guatemala

PCR Negative

But sailing with a stuffy nose,
sore throat, fuzzy mind, body
aches, and a swollen tongue
gives away to staring, eyes
sore in your head, a heightened
sense of breeze on skin, a sense
you're still in bed dreaming. North
of Dominican Republic passing
cliffs, small living lights, jungle,
the squalls on the radar feel
like sickness spots on my poor-
sick soul. The damp air, cloud-
filled sky remind me of a blanket
I should be under, cup of hot
soup in hand, favorite movie
on too late into the night. But,
a day of bashing against
the Atlantic to reach around,
out of Samana Bay, we missed
the whales, but connected with
family that had been held apart
for so long from Covid pandemic.
Swaying on this night's ocean
makes it seem so faraway. Head sail
bangs. Might jibe soon. Half
moon appears, disappears. Glows,
instead of shines. A calm in the soul.
Ache in the chest. Question
on the mind—gets stolen by a swell,
Selkie throws port—starboard,
settles—there's nothing but sea,
darkness, and a wondering like time,
a day that never seems to end, perhaps
being still in constant movement.
Is this home? Am I a sailor? Does my
inflatable vest fit? Will I swim?

Haiti

Reefed main. Reefed headsail.
We sail strong and fast straight
towards lightening. My body
attempts to rid itself of a cold
like the wind and waves try
to rid themselves of us. Fast
above ile de la tortue flying. Half
moon bright, behind pushes us
along sharing its dark side. Stars,
waves, wind take pity on us. Know
that we are under your control.
Lighthouse flicker. Lightening flash.
Lines squeak. The cloud's energy
is visual. Eight knots soaring towards
Cuba. The moon shines on the immense
swells of water that catch us. Push us.
There's a monster in me the sea wants
to expel. I can feel it gently breaking
giving me myself again.

Cuba

Below Guantanamo. Sailing.
Submarines in the area. Depths
read shallow. Strange. Storm
in the distance flashes silent
bright strings in the air. Wind—
steady. Waves—steady. Shadow
of Haiti lets us breath calmer
waters, but I think of the prisoners
in Guantanamo that can't see
these stars, this light show,
feel this breeze, and I know
without torture, they are punished
severely. Wing to wing, we flutter
softly over the surface with light
from the half empty moon. Quietly,
so as not to disturb opportunity.

Passing Jamaica

I'm gonna jump ship. Wash ashore,
wrap myself in black, green, yellow
and smoke a blunt. I'll take the crescent
moon rising above the lightening
clouds as my boat, arrive, and dance.
If we won't stop, I swear, I will jump
ship into the darkness of the night
waters, I won't be afraid. The salty
ocean will renew my skin and mind.
I'll tie my messy hair up and smile
at everyone I meet. I'll let the drums
change my heartbeat. The land change
my eyes, and the fruit change my hips.
No life jacket needed. I'll trust the current
to push me there, as I float under the stars
on blankets of jellyfish. Just watch.
This is the note I'll leave in the cockpit:
Don't worry, it will say. The Caribbean
Sea knows what to do with me, it told
me so. I could see the music rising
in the lights on the horizon. I saw
friendly faces in the darkness, jumping
ship was logical. It made the most sense.

Cayman Trench

Stars out. Storm passed. Moon
yet to rise. Darkness. The head sail bangs
on the pole to keep course. This night,
the first to see stars and not lightening,
is mostly quiet like we are badly tip-
toeing though a house with creaky,
wooden floor boards. It's better not to
disturb the depths of 20,000 feet.
That's deep. Where many questions sleep
waiting to be asked. I wiggle through
the Bimini hatch to see the Milky Way
spilled across the sky above. Ten degrees
might keep the sails more full—just
a bit. The Cayman Islands are blips
above us. They look like massive Cuba
has dropped some crumbs. More places
we don't get to see due to Covid. Is this
sailing or requesting—banging on doors?
Six days in. At least three to go. With
the vast trench below and the endless
space above, I proceed like the path
was made for us long ago. Lingering here
gives the feeling that this is the rest
—a calm night before a birthing.

Reflection

The crescent
moon is up. It knows
something
I don't.

Nicaraguan Rise

to avoid it
we jibe
back and forth
in the dark
contemplating
Honduran pirates
the lack of wind
our smallest child
with a fever
bobbing
rolling
sailing
adjusting
worrying on
our broken stay
loose rigging
vastness
of sea
if we will
encounter
the predicted winds
a deep red blowing visual
spreading from islands
to Central America
blushing at us
before
we left

Captain & 1st Mate

Like Romeo & Juliet, my husband
and I pass each other during the night
and then the day to relieve each other
of the watch. We cross paths briefly
with updates on wind, sails, squalls,
stars. He reaches his hand, rough
from the lines, as he descends into
the dim red-light glow of the cabin
to give me one last sense of together-
ness with a brush of his fingertips
across my leg, a silent love you,
a silent take care. Double-handed
couples get credit for crossing with
two, but parents slide under the radar,
disguised in numbers, crossing with
more difficulty than perceived. Tonight,
over a week, it gets too long. Nights
admiring stars and handling weather
become natural but lonely. Not even able
to dream next to one another, living
separately but within forty-nine feet.
He tells me to switch his cushion nest
to the low side, it's more comfy, he
says, a better view of the Milky Way.
I hesitate to move his cozy watch,
but do as suggested, and the stars spill
above my head, a dark, brilliant, speckled
dome that surrounds me from every
horizon as far as I can see, and I am
covered and held completely in his
arms, in his love. Just like one of our
first dates with a blanket, a beach,
some wine, and the stars. There is no
separation, no Shakespearean tragedy,
just another adventure where we are
patient enough to wait to hold each other
in a new place that we have sacrificed
time and togetherness to be even
closer together, to remain madly in love.

Wind

Like it was promised, arrives.
In the dark, its push is more
like a shove. The stars don't
notice. Innocent bystanders.

Aiming for Shelter

Around the lip of Tres Puntas,
just north of Livingston, the mouth
to Rio Dulce, we have been told
is a safe anchorage to wait
to enter the river. It is the land
of Tarzan, jungle walls that reach
high and thick, foliage so dense
that to approach parts of it afloat
will yield poisonous snakes seeking
refuge aboard, but now, a night
away, we take massive waves
that only the length of the whole
Caribbean Sea can build. In the dark,
the cockpit light reflects off a wall
of water that is sure to enter every
open hatch that we leave cracked
begging for air down below. Kids
sleep—oblivious—dreaming. I try,
myself, to help my husband,
by watching. It's too much. I wrap
my arms around my youngest
remembering the sounds, squeaks,
of a pod of blue whales' song
that followed us all morning and try
to sleep. Peace… His hand brushes
me awake again—my captain—
my husband. He's tired. I can feel
it in his touch. Then… the calm.
Swells that lift us gently in a night
breeze. Kindness. So close, we sail
the last fifty nautical miles able
to be thankful like Jane in the jungle,
we swing with ease, adapting
to our new home, shelter and care
central for living hurricane free—
Guatemala, twilight of our season.

Magdalena Hirt has a Master of Arts in English Literature from the University of Toledo and is currently working to receive her Master of Letters from the University of the Highlands and Islands in Orkney, Scotland. Her debut poetry chapbook, *Levels of the Ocean,* is available. She recently published articles in *Cruising World, Literary Traveler,* and *Enchanted Living.* Currently, she homeschools her four children and writes from her sailboat, which is a Westerly 49, named *Selkie.* Their family of six sails to circumnavigate the globe. She enjoys cooking and dancing—most of the time together. With pen, spatula, and helm in hand, her sailing soul belongs on the sea where she chooses words, academics, ingredients, and destinations. Follow their story at www.sealongingselkie.net.

www.ingramcontent.com/pod-product-compliance
Lightning Source LLC
Chambersburg PA
CBHW031126160426
43192CB00008B/1127